BEEN

ROG

THE SHAPES GAME

PICTURES BY
SIAN TUCKER

VERSE BY
PAUL ROGERS

ORCHARD BOOKS
London

For Judith Elliott
P.R.

To Jann and Tony
from Sian

Text copyright © Paul Rogers 1989
Illustrations copyright © Sian Tucker 1989
First published in Great Britain in 1989 by
ORCHARD BOOKS
96 Leonard Street, London EC2 4RH
Orchard Books Australia
14 Mars Road, Lane Cove NSW 2066
1 85213 143 8
Printed in Belgium

Shapes all around us.

Shall we play a game?

I'll spy a shape —

You say its name!

I spy a bubble,

A bouncy round ball,

A wheel shape, a sun shape,

A bang-the-big-bass-drum shape —

The shapes you see are all . . .

c i r c l e s

I spy a steeple,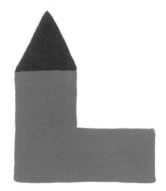

A gleaming Christmas tree,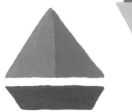

A sail shape, a cone shape,

A little pile of stones shape —

What shape can you see?

triangles

I spy a hanky,

A patch on someone's dress,

A tile shape, a dice shape,

A clinking-chunk-of-ice shape —

All are more or less . . .

square

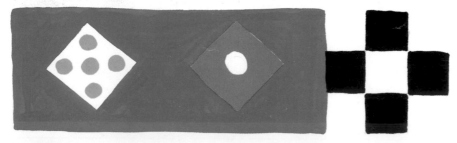

I spy a snowflake,

The flashing of a gem,

A flower shape, a spark shape,

A twinkle-in-the-dark shape —

What's the word for them?

s t a r s

I spy a bird's egg,

Leaves on the trees,

A prune shape, balloon shape,

A face-seen-in-a-spoon shape —

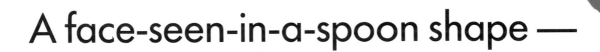

What are all of these?

o v a l s

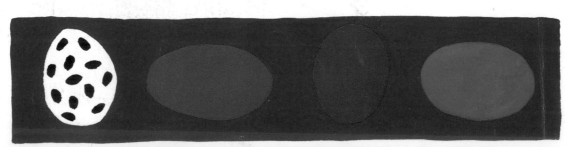

I spy a hammock,

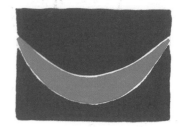

A slice of melon rind,

A smile shape, a skipping shape,

A fingernail-clipping shape —

Every one a kind of . . .

crescent

I spy a doorway,

A picture on the wall,

A window shape, a cage shape,

A look! — this-very-page shape —

These shapes we call . . .

rectangles

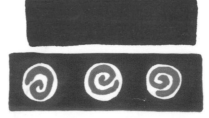

I spy a snailshell,

A twist of curly hair,

A drill shape, a screw shape,

A twirling-the-lasso shape —

Name the shapes there.

spirals

I spy a bright kite,

Dancing on the breeze,

A bird's-open-beak shape,

A not-allowed-to-peek shape —

What's the word for these?

diamonds

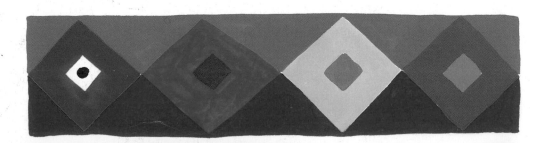

I spy a diamond,

A crescent and a star,

A spiral, circle, triangle,

An oval, square and rectangle —

Show me where they are.

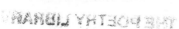

Shapes on the ceiling,

No two the same —

Quick — before they disappear —

Give them all a name!